The subje
vocabular
with exper
brief and simple text is printed
in large, clear type.

Children's questions are
anticipated and facts presented
in a logical sequence. Where
possible, the books show
what happened in the past
and what is relevant today.

Special artwork has been
commissioned to set a standard
rarely seen in books for this
reading age and at this price.

Full-colour illustrations are on
all 48 pages to give maximum
impact and provide the
extra enrichment that is the
aim of all Ladybird Leaders.

INDEX

For teachers' use, a map and geographical index is given at the back of the book.

A Ladybird Leader

apes
and monkeys

written and illustrated by John Leigh-Pemberton

Publishers: Ladybird Books Ltd . Loughborough
© Ladybird Books Ltd 1975
Printed in England

Primates

Apes and monkeys
belong to the same
animal group as
we do.

This group is
called the
'primates'.

'Primates' means
'top animals'.

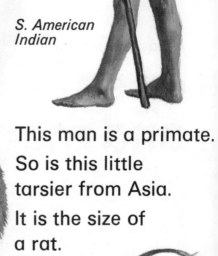

S. American
Indian

Tarsier

This man is a primate.
So is this little
tarsier from Asia.
It is the size of
a rat.

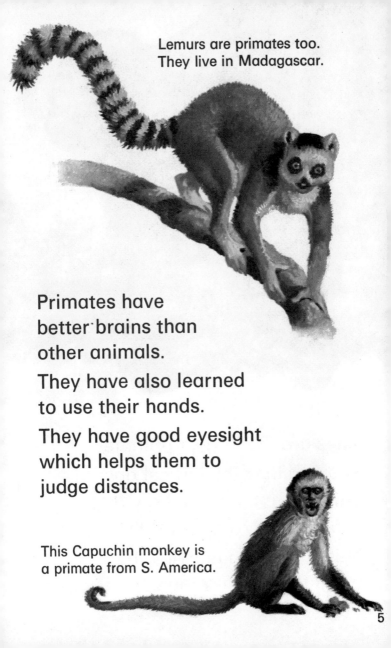

Lemurs are primates too.
They live in Madagascar.

Primates have
better brains than
other animals.

They have also learned
to use their hands.

They have good eyesight
which helps them to
judge distances.

This Capuchin monkey is
a primate from S. America.

5

Gorillas

Apes are the largest primates.
The gorilla is the largest ape.
They are 1.8 m (six feet) tall and
can weigh 270 kg (600 lb).
This is more than twice the
weight of a heavy man.

Some gorillas live in the thick
mountain forests of Central Africa.

Others live along the banks of
West African rivers like the Congo.

Gorillas form groups made up of
males and females, grown-ups
and young.

Gorillas — how they live

Gorillas are very powerful,
but they are quiet, shy animals.

They do not attack other
animals or man.

If they are attacked
they are very dangerous.

Gorillas eat only vegetable
matter such as leaves and fruit.

Every night they make leafy
nests in which the smaller
gorillas sleep.

Most of each day is spent in
eating or searching for food.

Chimpanzees

Chimpanzees live in tropical forests in Africa.

They are smaller, noisier, more active and more excitable than gorillas.

They usually live in mixed groups of not more than twenty.

Like other apes, chimpanzees
do not have tails.
Normally, they walk on all fours,
but, like other apes, they
can walk upright.
They are good climbers and
can run quite fast.

Chimpanzees are the most
intelligent of the apes.

They often become fierce
and destructive when grown up.

So, like all apes and monkeys,
they do not make good pets.

Chimpanzees eat mostly fruit,
berries and termites (an insect).

Sometimes they also kill and eat
other animals, including monkeys.

They make a new sleeping nest
every night, in about five minutes.

Orang-utan

This is a young one.
'Orang' means 'man'
and 'Utan' means
'jungle'.

Orang-utans are rare, shy apes,
found only in Sumatra and Borneo.

They have very long arms and,
when old, become very heavy.

Usually they live alone or in
pairs with their young.

This is an old male. He may weigh as much as 100 kg (220 lb).

They inhabit thick forest and spend almost all their lives in the trees.

Fruit is their chief food.

Gibbons

Apes do not have tails or
bare patches on their bottoms,
as Asian and African
monkeys do.

Apes are bigger and more
intelligent than monkeys.

Somewhere in between the
apes and monkeys are
animals called gibbons.

Gibbons are intelligent.
They have no tails, but
they do have bare patches
on their bottoms.

They live in the trees
in the jungles of
South East Asia.

They are wonderful
acrobats and are
very noisy.

A gibbon's arm is
twice the length of
its body.

Langurs — leaf-eating monkeys

There are two groups of monkeys.

The New World monkeys
live in South America.

The Old World monkeys
live in Asia and Africa.

*Golden langur
from the Himalayas.*

The rare Douc langur from South East Asia.

There are more than
fifty kinds of Old World monkeys.

Some of the most numerous
and largest are the langurs.

They are found from the
Himalayas to Borneo.

Colobus monkeys

Colobus or Guereza monkeys
live in Africa.

They come from the same
family as the langurs
of Asia.

They were once much hunted
for their beautiful long fur.

These monkeys live in family
groups among the large trees
of thick forests.

They eat very tough leaves.

To digest these they have
a special kind of stomach.

Colobus babies are white when born.

Macaques — 'dog-faced' monkeys

Macaques are found in Asia,
Japan and North Africa.

Like some other Old World
monkeys, they have cheek
pouches in which they collect food.

Japanese macaque

*Rhesus macaque
from S. Asia.*

Some live in cold places
and have quite long fur.

They eat all sorts of food.

The Barbary macaque

The Barbary 'ape' is the only monkey found in Europe.

Some live on the Rock of Gibraltar and some in North Africa.

The Barbary ape has no tail.

Macaques inhabit cliffs and trees.

They are good swimmers.

Most of them have short tails.

Mangabeys — 'white-eyelid' monkeys

Mangabeys are big monkeys which live in tropical African forests.

They live in large groups.

Like all other monkeys and apes, they usually have one baby at a time.

Twins are sometimes born.

Red-capped mangabey. These monkeys carry their long tails curled over their backs.

Guenons — 'long-tailed' monkeys

There are many different kinds of guenons in Africa.

They live in forest or grassland.

They form large, noisy groups.

Vervet monkey

Diana monkey

Owl-faced monkey

Moustached monkey

Baboons

Large herds of baboons live in Africa among rocks or in grassland.

They eat roots, insects and honey.

Baboons are powerful monkeys with large teeth.

They call with a deep bark.

Few other animals will attack them.

'Sacred' baboons

Female with young.

Male

Baby apes and monkeys are carried about by their mothers.

Mandrill

The blue cheeks
are made of bone.

Mandrills are related to baboons,
but they live in tropical forests
and not in open country.

These very powerful animals eat
nuts, fruit and grubs.

Titi monkey

Saki

South American monkeys

South American monkeys
look rather like the Asian
and African monkeys,
but they are not very
closely related to them.

They are different in
many ways.

These monkeys do not have
bare patches on their bottoms.

They have no cheek pouches
as Old World monkeys do.

Some of them can use
their tails to grip with.

*Spider
monkey*

Red howler monkeys

Monkey voices

Most monkeys live in groups.

A group lives in part of
a forest or jungle.

This is their 'territory'.

The territory contains their
food and the trees they
live in.

Monkeys use their voices to defend their territory.

Their cries keep them in touch with the rest of their group.

Some bark like dogs or chirp like birds.

Some hoot.

Howler monkeys live in tropical S. American forests. They howl or roar like a lion. The sound can be heard for miles.

Black howler

Uakaris

Uakaris are quiet, shy monkeys.
They are about the size of a cat.
They live in the Amazon
forests of Brazil.
They are becoming quite rare
because the local people eat them.

Uakaris blush
bright red
when angry
or excited.

Squirrel monkeys

Little squirrel monkeys are very plentiful throughout most of South America.

They live in large bands, often as many as a hundred in a group. Their tails are not 'prehensile'.

'Prehensile' means that the tail can be used to grip with.

Capuchin or Ring-tail monkey

Capuchins live in South America.
They are perhaps the most
intelligent of all monkeys.

They use stones to crack nuts,
and defend themselves with sticks.

This is the monkey most often
kept in captivity.

Douroucouli or Night ape

Monkeys are day-time animals.
The word for this is 'diurnal'.
The South American Douroucouli
is the only monkey which is
active at night.
The word for this is 'nocturnal'.

Woolly monkeys

Some South American monkeys
hardly ever leave the trees.

But the woolly monkeys come
down to the ground and walk
on their hind legs.

They are quite large, with
grey, black or brown fur.

There are no apes in S. America.

But there are seventy kinds
of monkeys and marmosets.

They live from Mexico to the
north-eastern part of Argentina.

Woolly monkeys live in the
huge Amazon forests.

Hands and feet

Monkeys use their feet as well as their hands for gripping.

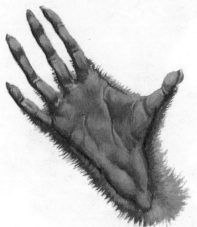

A monkey foot. The back of hands and feet are usually covered with fur.

Some kinds of monkeys do not have thumbs.

These monkeys use their hands like hooks.

Monkey hand

No thumb

The tail used as a balance when a monkey makes a leap.

Tails

All monkeys use their tails to help them to balance.

This is specially so with monkeys which live in the trees.

Some New World monkeys can grip with their tails.

These 'prehensile' tails have a bare patch at the tip.

The pad at the end of a prehensile tail.

Silvery marmoset

Marmosets usually have twin babies. Sometimes three are born.

Common marmoset

Marmosets

There are thirty-three different kinds of marmosets.

They are dwarf monkeys which live in the Amazon forests.

They have sharp claws to help them climb and move like squirrels.

Some marmosets have ear tufts,
beards or moustaches.

Their voices are so high that
sometimes they cannot be heard
by humans.

Marmosets feed mostly on fruit,
eggs and insects.

They live in families or
in small groups.

Pygmy marmosets

The bodies
of Pygmy marmosets
are only 102 mm
(four inches) long.
They are the
smallest primates.

Tamarins

Tamarins are marmosets which
have two teeth like tusks
in their lower jaw.

They live in tropical forests
from Panama to southern Brazil.

There are twenty different kinds.

Golden lion tamarin.
It is the size
of a squirrel.

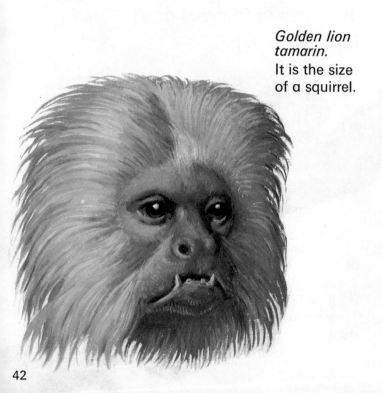

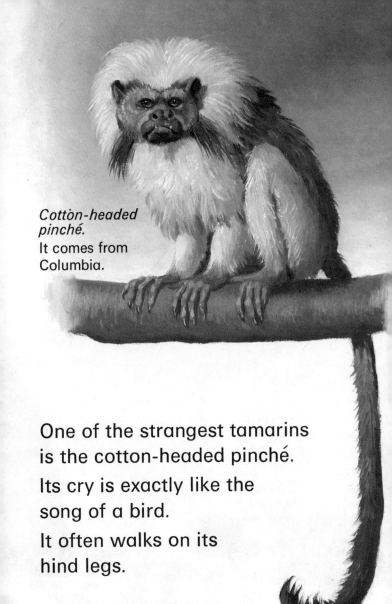

Cotton-headed pinché.
It comes from Columbia.

One of the strangest tamarins is the cotton-headed pinché.

Its cry is exactly like the song of a bird.

It often walks on its hind legs.

43

Lemurs

Lemurs are primates — distant
relations of the monkeys.

Once they were the 'top animals'
in Africa, Europe, Asia and
in America.

When other animals became
stronger and cleverer the lemurs
began to disappear.

Now they are found only
in Madagascar.

Madagascar is an island which
was cut off from the African
mainland fifty million
years ago.
The lemurs were stranded there.

The ring-tailed lemur

This is the commonest lemur.

It lives among rocks and eats mostly fruit and insects.

It is about the size of a cat.

Ring-tailed lemur

Mouse lemur

Some more lemurs

The mouse lemur is
only 127 mm (five inches) long.

It is a fierce little animal.

Like other lemurs, the squirrel
lemur is becoming rare.

This is because the forests where
they live are
being destroyed.

Squirrel lemur

Grooming

Animals like monkeys and lemurs
groom and clean each other's fur.

This is called 'social grooming'.

To do this, lemurs have special
teeth in the front of their
lower jaw.

They work rather like a comb.

The red-ruffed lemur
is as big as a fox.
It lives among tall
forest trees.

Sifaka

Sifakas and indris

Sifakas and indris
are large, rare lemurs
which live in the trees.

They have dog-like
faces and bark
like dogs too.

After a huge meal of leaves the
sifaka gives a loud hiccup — 'she-fak'.
This is how it got its name.

Indris

Powerful hind limbs
help sifakas and indris to
make enormous leaps
from tree to tree.

They grip the branches with
their extra large big toes.

The smaller lemurs take the place
of monkeys in Madagascar.

The indris takes the place of the apes.

The slender loris from India and Sri Lanka. It is a slow and cautious mover.

Some small primates

The primate group of mammals includes several small creatures. Although they do not look much like monkeys or men they are distantly related to them.

The African galago or bush baby. It is a great acrobat and has a cry like that of a human child.

The tarsier.
It comes from parts
of S.E. Asia.
Special pads on its
fingers and toes help
it to grip any surface.

These little primates
are nocturnal and live
in the trees.

Special hands and feet like
pincers help them to grip
the branches.

They eat bird's eggs, insects,
flowers, leaves and fruit.

The potto.
This African animal
has sharp spines on the
back of its neck.

World distribution of apes and monkeys

NORTH AMERICA

Gibraltar

Mexico

Trinidad

Equator

River Amazon

Peru

Brazil

SOUTH AMERICA

River (Con

Argentina

S A H

A

Old World monkeys
(only baboons in Arabia,
only barbary apes in Europe - *Gibraltar*

New World monkeys and marmosets